IT HAPPENED TO ME

Being BULLIED

Stories from Survivors

SARAH EASON

CHERITON CHILDREN'S BOOKS

Published in 2026 by **Cheriton Children's Books**
1 Bank Drive West, Shrewsbury, Shropshire, SY3 9DJ, UK

First Edition

Author: Sarah Eason
Designer: Paul Myerscough
Illustrator: Sylwia Filipczak
Editor: Ella Newby
Proofreader: Rachel Kenney

Picture credits: Cover: Sylwia Filipczak. Inside: p4: Shutterstock/LightField Studios, p5: Shutterstock/Creativa Images, p6: Shutterstock/M. Rohana, p8: Shutterstock/Daniel Hoz, p9: Shutterstock/Pixel Shot, p10: Shutterstock/Fizkes, p13: Shutterstock/Oneinchpunch, p14: Shutterstock/Monkey Business Images, p15: Shutterstock/PeopleImages.com/Yuri A, p16: Shutterstock/Motortion Films, p19: Shutterstock/Fast Stock, p20: Shutterstock/PeopleImages.com/Yuri A, p23: Shutterstock/SmLyubov, p24: Shutterstock/F01 Photo, p25: Shutterstock/Pornchai Oom, p26: Shutterstock/Golubovy, p28: Shutterstock/PeopleImages.com/Yuri A, p30: Shutterstock/PeopleImages.com/Yuri A, p32: Shutterstock/VH Studio, p34: Shutterstock/Halfpoint, p36: Shutterstock/DimaBerlin, p39: Shutterstock/Tutatamafilm, p40: Shutterstock/VH Studio, p42: Shutterstock/Jacob Lund, p43: Shutterstock/2xSamara.com, p44: Shutterstock/Thomas Andreas.

Printed in China

Publisher's Note: The stories in this book are fictional stories based on extensive research of real-life experiences. The photographs of people included throughout are used for illustrative purposes only. The publishers do not suggest that the people featured have any of the conditions discussed in the book.

CONTENTS

CHAPTER ONE

WHEN A PERSON IS BULLIED

Bullying can happen to anyone, anywhere. Many people are bullied at some time in their life, but it is never their fault. It is not because of what they do or how they behave. The reason bullying happens is all about the bully. People who bully use what they think is their power to upset or control others. They may be bigger or stronger than their victims, and they use that to bully them. They may be more popular than the people they bully, and use that as a means to gain control over them. Whatever the cause or focus of the bullying, it is wrong. Bullying should never be tolerated.

WHAT IS BULLYING?

It is important to clearly identify what bullying is. When someone is in a bad mood and calls a friend a name, that is not necessarily bullying. If someone accidentally pushes another person, that one incident does not count as bullying either. Bullying is when someone intends to hurt another person, and either keeps on doing it or intends to keep on doing it. If someone hurts another person accidentally, it is annoying and they should say sorry. But it does not make them a bully. If a friend is mean, they should apologize too. But if it doesn't happen over and over then hopefully it can be resolved. In contrast, bullies are consistently aggressive, and repeatedly do things to hurt someone else. That is what makes bullying so painful, so difficult to manage, and so serious.

Being bullied is a truly horrible experience that can leave people feeling frightened and alone.

HURTFUL AND SCARY

Bullying comes in many forms, but essentially, bullying is when someone does something to hurt, scare, or threaten another person on purpose, time and again. Most of us have seen bullying, or had the misfortune to experience bullying, at some time in our lives. Just a few examples of bullying are when someone keeps pushing another person around, spreads false stories about them, or insults them when they walk past, and encourages others to do so too.

Despite recent campaigns to try and end bullying, it remains a serious problem.

It Happened to Me

This book follows the "It Happened to Me" fictional journals of different young people who have been bullied. These stories from survivors explain what impact bullying had on them. The conclusions to their stories on pages 44–45 show that it is possible to overcome bullying and lead a happy and fulfilling life. The stories and information in this book can support people who are being bullied and help everyone better understand what it is like to be in this situation.

DIFFERENT TYPES OF BULLYING

There are three main types of bullying. Verbal bullying is when a bully says or writes mean things to or about someone else. It can include name-calling, **taunting**, and threatening. A lot of the bullying that goes on in school is verbal. There is also relationship or social bullying. This happens when a bully or group of bullies excludes someone on purpose. They tell other people not to be friends with them, and spread rumors, or false stories, about them. They may also do or say things in public that embarrass someone, for example, revealing their secrets. The third type of bullying is physical.

PHYSICAL BULLYING

In physical bullying, the main weapon the bully uses is their body. They might shove, punch, or kick someone, or they might damage their belongings. Sometimes, the physical bully leaves their victim with cuts, bruises, or other injuries. Often, though, physical bullying includes actions such as pulling someone's hair or clothes, or pinching or pushing them. While this may not leave marks that anyone can see, it is still physical bullying.

Physical bullying can be very frightening for victims, who dread often-daily attacks.

A recent study by Pew Research Center found that 21 percent of Black teens have experienced online bullying centered around their race. That included cyberbullying, which often included offensive name-calling. The bullying also involved spreading rumors about the teens who were targeted.

TARGETS FOR BULLYING

People bully all kinds of people for many different reasons. However, unfortunately some groups of people may be at an increased risk of being bullied. That is because bullies see them as different in some way. Bullies are often mean and destructive toward people who are more obviously different from themselves. Those differences may include race, religion, or **disability**. For example, bullies may target people of a different racial background, such as Black or Latino people. They often pick on people who have a different religion, such as Muslim, Sikh, or Jewish people. They may also single out people with disabilities, both physical and mental. When someone bullies another person because of their race, religion, culture, or disability it is called **prejudice**. Bullies also sometimes target people they think look weak or unlikely to fight back. They may focus on people who look nervous or have low **self-esteem**.

IT HAPPENS

In 2018, a Sikh student in Texas was targeted on the school bus by his **peers**. They called him a **terrorist** and made fun of his **turban**. And in 2019, in a Los Angeles high school, a Jewish student found **swastikas** drawn on his locker. He was also taunted about the concentration camps used by the **Nazis** during World War II (1939–1945). These are just two of the many examples of religion-based bullying of teens in recent years.

They might shove, punch, or kick someone ...

WHAT MAKES A BULLY?

Very often, bullies are people who have, in fact, been bullied themselves. A bully may be someone who has a hard time at home, and does not feel loved or cared for by their family. When someone is bullied, shouted at constantly, or even hurt at home, they may take out their anger and frustration by bullying someone at school. They are repeating ways of behaving that they have learned at home. Sometimes, they bully others as a way to get attention for their own suffering at the hands of a bully.

FEELING LOW, ACTING STRONG

Some people bully because they lack self-confidence or self-esteem. They may seem confident and loud, but actually, they do not feel very powerful. By bullying someone they perceive as weaker than themselves, they may feel that they look more powerful and confident. There are also other reasons why people bully, which include:

- ***Wanting to Fit In:*** In some cases, individuals bully to fit in with a group or be more popular. They may believe that bullying makes them more popular or helps them avoid being bullied themselves.

When bullying behavior is not dealt with and there are no consequences for such actions, people may continue to bully because they have no fear of any punishment.

- ***Lack of Understanding:*** Some bullies may not fully understand or care about the pain they are causing. This lack of **empathy** can come from emotional or **psychological** issues. They may also not be particularly sensitive toward the feelings of others.
- ***Emotional or Psychological Problems:*** People who bully may be dealing with mental health problems or emotional issues such as anger, frustration, or **anxiety**. Bullying becomes a way to express those feelings, even though it is wrong.

Bullies target individuals they believe they can have some power over, often using many different means to attack them. Sadly, modern technology has made it easier than ever to bully.

IT HAPPENS

A bully may feel jealous of someone's success, appearance, or other positive things in their life. They may bully that person as a way to undermine them or punish them because they are envious of the good things in their life.

"I knew I was being mean when I bullied, but at the time it made me feel good. I was in control, not the other way around."

Everyone Is Scared of Them

THURSDAY APRIL 17

It happened again at school today. They waited for me at lunch, then followed me wherever I went—it was impossible to get away from them. They just kept walking after me and calling me names. Everyone stared at me, but no one did anything to help. Some of them even laughed. Jenny and Claudia looked really uncomfortable about it. They used to be friendly with me, but now they steer clear—have done ever since Tina and her friends started picking on me. Everyone is scared of them.

MONDAY MAY 12

Tina snatched my bag today and looked inside it. Pulled everything out. She laughed when she looked at my pencil case, and said it was for nerdy babies. All her friends laughed too. She said she was keeping it, so she could show everyone what a loser I am. I asked her to give it back, but she just laughed and threw my bag back at me. Keeping it, she said. I had to go back into class with no pens. I asked Mrs Cooke for one. She said that's not like me, but gave me a pen. I wish I could tell her about what is happening to me, but I don't dare.

I wish it would end, but I don't know how to stop it.

WEDNESDAY JUNE 4

Today was horrible and I couldn't wait to get home. It's the only place where I think they can't get to me. But even then, they find a way–through my phone. I know I shouldn't look, but I can't help it. It's like I have to know what they are saying about me. But when I do look, it's even worse. I can see all the comments they have made. Weirdo. Loser. Psycho. I stare at the words, and think that is all anyone sees now when they look at me.

FRIDAY JUNE 13

I could see Tina picking on someone else today, another girl. She looked really scared. She is new at school. Tina kept pushing her, and then she grabbed her bag too. I saw her take something out of it. I wanted to do something, to stop her, but I felt too scared. Tina saw me looking, so she came over to me and asked if I had a problem.

She said I must feel left out. Then she shoved me against the wall and said she had plenty of time for me too. Tina didn't know it, but Mrs Cooke came round the corner just then. She shouted at Tina to stop what she was doing. Tina looked really shocked–she is normally super careful not to get caught, but this time she lost out.

Tina was marched straight to Mrs Cooke's office. Afterward, she came to find me and told me that Tina had been sent to the principal's office. Mrs Cooke asked me what had been going on. I knew she wasn't going to let it go, so I told her the truth, about Tina and the others. She said she hated bullying, and the school would not **tolerate** it. She told me I didn't need to be scared anymore–the bullying stopped here.

CHAPTER TWO

BULLYING AND THE TEENAGE YEARS

The teenage years are often difficult by their nature. With puberty comes a lot of hormonal changes, which can make people feel up and down emotionally. And during this choppy time, teens are still learning how to manage their emotions, too. Feelings of anger, frustration, jealousy, or inadequacy can make people feel overwhelmed at times. That may make some people lash out at others through bullying, as a way to deal with these difficult emotions. Insecurity and struggling to find one's identity are also common parts of adolescence, which can make some people easier targets for bullying.

A TROUBLESOME TEENAGE TIME

During adolescence, people are finding out who they are. Some teens may want to experiment with their appearance and behavior in ways that do not necessarily fit in with what many other teens consider "normal." For example, they may dye or style their hair differently, or wear clothes that other teens think are weird. They may want to try out interests and hobbies that other teens wouldn't consider. Everyone is different, and it is good to try different things to find out what you like. However, sadly, for some teens this experimental time can make them vulnerable to both **peer pressure** and judgment. Added to that, during this phase, they may also feel insecure about their appearance, abilities, or how popular they are. That makes them vulnerable to bullying behavior.

The National Center for Education Statistics (NCES) reports that around 20 percent of students aged 12–18 have experienced bullying at school.

Teens may feel under a lot of pressure to conform, or fit in, with what other teens see as "normal."

IT HAPPENS

The up-and-down hormonal shifts that teens experience can cause frequent and extreme mood swings. At this time of life, emotions can feel far more intense than at most other life stages. That can make some people behave in ways they later regret. Those behaviors include bullying.

UNDER PRESSURE

There is also a lot of pressure on teens to be part of a group, and many young people desperately want to fit in. Adolescents may join in with bullying to try and fit in with a certain group or to avoid being bullied themselves. Sometimes, teens join in with bullying because they fear being left out or becoming a target themselves if they don't conform to group behavior.

For teens, schools, peer groups, and social circles often have clear **hierarchies**. And there are always teens who have more power and influence within those hierarchies than others. Teens at the top may bully those lower down to keep their position. By showing others they are tough and strong, they are less likely to be challenged. Bullying can also be a way to climb the ladder to the top of the group too, and take charge of it.

FRIENDSHIPS AND BULLYING

When bullying affects relationships such as friendships, it can be extremely upsetting. An example of relationship bullying is when someone invites everyone in the class except one person to a party. Another is when they find reasons to exclude someone in other ways. When people who are meant to be friends start whispering about someone behind their back, that is bullying. If they suddenly become quiet when a person walks by, as if they are talking about them, that is bullying. Relationship bullying can make people feel left out, lonely, and extremely insecure. It can be really hurtful, and damaging.

What is especially nasty about relationship bullying is that while it may be started by one person, other people join in or let it happen. It can feel as if the people someone thought were friends now dislike them. The truth is that even good people can make mistakes sometimes, and go along with bullying. They often do it because they are scared that if they don't, they themselves will be bullied.

If you or someone you know is being bullied, always tell a trusted adult.

"I was never popular at school. When the bullying started, and they called me a freak, I began to believe it."

IT HAPPENED TO THEM

There are many examples of successful people who were bullied as teens. Taylor Swift is one of them. The Grammy-winning superstar says she was left out and often bullied because of her love of country music and her ambition to become a performing artist. Taylor usually ate her lunch alone at school, and was rarely treated as part of a group. Due to her own experiences of bullying, the star today uses her fame to speak out about bullying and encourage other young people to do the same. She has even written about the bullying she experienced in her songs.

THE PROBLEM WITH COMPARISONS

Comparisons among teens can be a source of bullying, especially among friendships and other peer groups. Teens are often exploring who they are, and comparing themselves with others. That includes what they look like and how they behave. It includes their likes and dislikes. It also includes the other people that they choose to hang out with. People often feel under intense pressure to fit in with the group. They may also be encouraged to single out people who do not seem to fit in. That can easily lead to bullying.

It's normal to want to feel part of a group—it's human nature. However, taking part in bullying in order to remain part of a group is never acceptable.

Cyberbullying is extremely cruel and harmful. No one should take part in it, whether that is posting messages or photos or reacting to them.

TEENS AND CYBERBULLYING

Cyberbullying has become a real problem today, because the readily available access to technology makes it even easier to send mean and rude messages to or about another person. The messages are sent with the intention of making that person feel embarrassed or upset. Cyberbullies also use technology to harass or threaten another person. This type of bullying can be devastating because victims feel they have no escape from it. At one time, before technology such as cell phones, people who were bullied at school could at least feel safe when they got home. Today, victims of cyberbullying face constant **stress**. Many of us use our cell phones, tablets, and computers all the time. That means that once bullies get access to someone online, they can target them day and night.

"I try to block them, but they just get a new account and start again. It's like it will never end!"

HIDING BEHIND THE TECH

Another cruel and difficult truth about cyberbullying is that it is often anonymous. That means the person carrying out the bullying does it secretly, without revealing their identity. The target of the bullying may not know who sent a mean text to them, or posted an embarrassing photo of them. This can make cyberbullies lose control, and be even more extreme with their bullying. They cannot see the effects of their bullying on other people as they would if they were bullying at school, so they become even meaner online. They feel they are safe bullying people online, and less likely to be caught.

A PLACE TO BE CRUEL

Many people use social networking sites such as Facebook, Instagram, X, and Snapchat every day. These sites can be great. People get to discuss things like music and news, post images and articles about themselves, and comment on other people's profiles. But the sites are also places where cyberbullies can be extremely cruel. A cyberbully can hack into a person's account. They can then post embarrassing photographs on their account, making it seem like the account owner put them there. Some cyberbullies post insulting or hurtful messages on other people's profile pages. They may also put unpleasant images of someone on their own page and link it to all their friends, to upset their victim.

In recent years, bullying among teens has become a growing concern, especially with the rise of cyberbullying. For example, a 2023 survey found that 26.5 percent of teens reported experiencing cyberbullying within the previous 30 days. That was a significant increase from previous years. Common forms of cyberbullying include hurtful comments, rumors, and exclusion from online groups. Nearly 20 percent of teens reported staying home from school due to bullying. That shows the enormous impact that bullying has on mental health and school attendance.

WHEN BULLIES ARE OLDER

Bullies are usually around the same age as their targets. So, if bullying happens at school, the chances are that the bully and the person who is being bullied are in the same class, or year. Sometimes, however, adults can be bullies too. Most of the parents, teachers, coaches, and other adults involved with teens are kind, caring, and want what is best for the young people they are involved with. However, sometimes unacceptable behavior by adults does take place, and it can be classified as bullying.

PARENTS WHO BULLY

Most parents get a little mad sometimes. It may be that their children have done something to anger them. It is not bullying if a parent scolds a child for not doing their chores again and again, or if they tell them what to do. Most parents only get mad because they care about their kids and want them to be the best they can be. However, some parents bully their kids. A parent who bullies is someone who **abuses** their child in some way. Bullying by parents can take a number of forms.

USING CRUEL WORDS AND MANIPULATION

Parents who bully may insult their children. That can include telling them that they are stupid or useless. It can include name-calling, too. Some parents **manipulate** their children by withholding their love and support. They may do so if their child does something they do not like, or they may try to make them earn approval and love. They may also "gaslight" their children. This means manipulating them in such a way that they find it difficult to trust what they think and feel. For example, if a child is upset about the way a parent is behaving and tells them, the parent may say they are overreacting, and dismiss them. That makes the child feel confused and that they are not justified in feeling as they do.

Adults who were emotionally bullied by their parents during childhood are much more likely to suffer from mental health issues. A recent study by the *Journal of the American Medical Association (JAMA)* found that those who had suffered emotional bullying in childhood were 50 percent more likely to have **depression** or anxiety.

Sometimes parents bully their children by constantly criticizing them.

IT HAPPENS

Some parent bullies even hit, or threaten to hit, their children. Physical abuse can be shown as hitting, kicking, or physically harming a child in another way. The **trauma** experienced by children and young people from such abuse can be very difficult to deal with and overcome.

USING HUMILIATION AND CONTROL

Parents who bully may also put down their children by embarrassing them in front of others, including their friends and family. They may make jokes at their expense. Mocking children and belittling, or putting them down, is also a way of bullying. Controlling every aspect of their child's life, without consideration for their thoughts, feelings, or need for independence is another way that parents bully.

"From 5 to 15 years old I was belittled or ignored. They made me feel like I wasn't worth anything."

Some parent bullies even hit, or threaten to hit, their children.

TROUBLE WITH TEACHERS

Young people navigating their teenage years often experience a lot of complex emotions related to how they see themselves and how they feel about themselves. At this important stage of life a teen may feel embarrassed, hurt, or angry when a teacher criticizes them in front of the whole class. They may feel upset if they are punished for doing something wrong. But neither instances are necessarily bullying. It is a teacher's job to keep their class under control, and to ensure that their students do their work on time and try their best. They do this to help students achieve good results, and learn the correct way to behave in certain situations. Sometimes, though, a teacher uses their position of power in a negative way, and this behavior becomes bullying.

HOW DO TEACHERS BULLY?

Teens are often discovering how they feel about important issues for the first time. A teacher is a bully if they regularly pick on one student, criticizing them and putting them down, often for no reason. Perhaps they make fun of that student, mocking them for their work, race, personality, or appearance, and making the rest of the class laugh at them. Or they could consistently grade their work lower than the student truly feels they deserve. Some teachers may even hit their students, or threaten to hit them.

A good coach always focuses on positive encouragement to motivate their players.

PRESSURE IN SPORT

It can get pretty intense on a sports field. Emotions run high, especially during important games. Coaches are often seen on the sidelines, shouting to their players to run faster, work harder, and focus. Tough coaching is about positively pushing a player out of their comfort zone, to make them better. Coaches demand focus and effort every day, during practice as well as in a competition. Sometimes a coach may tease or say something slightly mean to a player to make them work harder. However, they must be careful not to cross a line and become a bully.

IT HAPPENS

Some people think that bullying behavior by coaches is motivational, or designed to encourage the people they are coaching. They think that shouting at someone or calling them a failure will make them work harder. But if a coach is constantly calling the players on their team rude or mean names, that is bullying. If a coach always yells at their players, they are a bully. And if a coach constantly belittles or insults players, they are a bully. When a coach is a bully, they can make a student hate a sport they used to love. It can make them so unhappy that it affects their life more generally. It is damaging to the person being bullied, and it also produces worse results on the sports field.

If a coach constantly belittles or insults players, they are a bully.

Dad's a Bully

TUESDAY FEBRUARY 11

Dad has gone away this week. I can tell Mom is relieved—me too. It's so much better when he isn't here. She is happier. I'm happier. We can both just breathe a bit, and relax.

But he couldn't go without being mean, could he? Told me to try and do something meaningful this week, like get my grades up. He said it wouldn't hurt to maybe try and get a job, instead of lazing around. It's like he can't help himself. He can't say anything nice. Just had to get a final dig in before he went. Mom raised her eyebrows at me as he shut the door. We've got the house to ourselves for a week, she smiled. I wish it was forever.

FRIDAY FEBRUARY 14

Dad's come back early. He said the conference was cut short because of the weather. I'm trying to keep out of his way. It's OK while I'm at school, but he's working at home more these days, so he is often there when I get back. He says the same thing every night: Anything good to tell me? Probably not, never is, is there? Well, at least I'm managing my expectations. It would be great to have a son who actually achieves something once in a while, though. Maybe you'll surprise me someday and come home with an A. Then he snorts, laughs, and says he's just kidding. But I know he's not. He really means every word.

Mom tells him to stop it. But he tells her she needs to find her sense of humor. She doesn't think it's any funnier than I do. He picks on her too. Dad's a bully.

MONDAY MARCH 17

It's parent-teacher conference tonight. Dad told me he is coming with Mom, and wants to hear all about my grand achievements at school. Said it's the highlight of his year.

I begged Mom to stop him from coming. She said she really tried, but he insisted on it. She said she'll stop him from saying anything, but I know she can't. He always does it, every year. It's so embarrassing. He doesn't get how it makes the teachers embarrassed, makes all of us embarrassed. They can't believe he is my dad, I know it. I can see it from the looks on their faces. Dads aren't supposed to talk about their kids like that.

Mr Penn was great tonight. Straight off, Dad told him he wasn't expecting much—just to let him know before we got into it. Unless something miraculous had happened since last time, I was still just about getting through, right? Nothing to shout home about. Mr Penn said, actually, my grades were fine, I was doing great, everything was going well. Then he made a point of saying, your son is a pleasure to teach. He kind of gave Dad a firm look when he said that.

Dad didn't know what to say—for once. I could have hugged Mr Penn. Mom looked so happy, like she was going to burst with pride. I love Mom. Just wish she'd stand up to Dad more. But she's scared.

When we got back, Dad said he was off again tomorrow, on another work trip. Mom gave me a hug. She said she was so proud of me, and we'd talk more in the morning.

CHAPTER THREE

THE DANGERS OF BULLYING

Bullying can severely damage both physical and emotional health. On an emotional level, bullying affects people's self-esteem. They can lose confidence and start to think that, in some way, the bullying is their fault. They may feel that they are all alone, and that there is nothing they can do about it. They often believe that no one would understand how they feel if they told them.

FEELING DEPRESSED

Teens who are bullied are at a higher risk of developing depression. Feelings of sadness, hopelessness, and worthlessness can result from the bullying, which can deepen into depression. When teens are depressed they often show a lack of interest in activities they would normally enjoy.

WORRYING ALL THE TIME

Bullying often causes a lot of anxiety and stress. Teens may feel constantly on edge. They are likely to worry a lot about when they will next be bullied. They often fear social situations that could make them vulnerable to bullying. This constant anxiety can cause problems with concentration. Teens may try and stay home to avoid finding themselves in a situation in which they could be bullied.

Bullying can make people feel very scared, upset, and alone.

According to the Anxiety and Depression Association of America (ADAA), panic attacks are increasingly common among adolescents.

Bullying can be so mentally destructive that it causes panic attacks in some people.

That then results in them feeling **isolated**. They may even suffer from panic attacks. These are very frightening episodes in which people feel they cannot breathe properly. They may have heart palpitations, sweat, and tremble. They can also feel dizzy and sick, among other symptoms, or signs.

"It got so bad that I stopped going out. There was always a chance that they could find me. It wasn't worth taking the risk."

IT HAPPENS

Sometimes, bullying can result in a condition known as post-traumatic stress disorder (PTSD). When a person has PTSD, they may relive the traumatic event as if it is happening again. They may have recurring nightmares about it. They can feel constantly on-edge, as if the event could occur again at any time. PTSD can be so far-reaching that it affects a person's ability to go to school, work, and have relationships.

BULLIES CAUSE SICKNESS

The negative effects of bullying can literally make people sick. People who experience bullying often suffer from a number of health issues. Some of those problems include:

- ***Problems Fighting Bugs*:** When the body is under stress over a long period of time, the **immune system** becomes suppressed, or reduced. That makes it more likely that people will catch infections, such as colds.
- ***Gut Issues:*** Stress can also result in many intestinal problems such as abdominal pain. People may experience changes in their appetite. They may struggle to eat, and then lose weight. Alternatively, some people eat more in an attempt to comfort themselves with food. They may gain weight as a result.
- ***Tiredness and Aches and Pains:*** Long-term stress can result in extreme exhaustion. People may lack the energy to do normal activities, and be unable to do things they once enjoyed. They may also experience pain in their muscles, often caused by **tension**. Muscle pain and headaches are common symptoms of a person experiencing bullying.

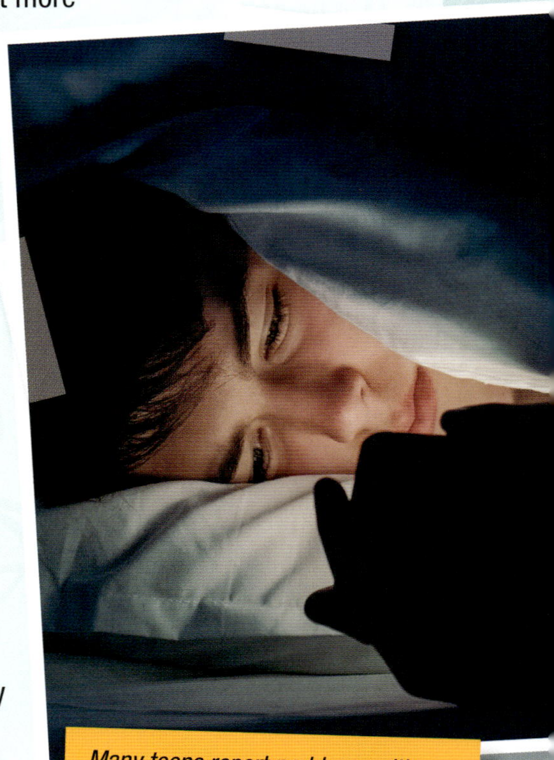

Many teens report problems with sleeping when experiencing bullying.

Victims of bullying are at risk of self-harm. A study published in *The Lancet Psychiatry* found that adolescents who were bullied were three to five times more likely to carry out self-harm compared to those who were not bullied.

- ***Problems with Sleep:*** People who are very anxious and stressed often find it difficult to sleep well. They may have trouble getting to sleep or staying asleep. Chronic, or long-lasting, stress and lack of sleep can then cause feelings of exhaustion. That makes it very difficult to wake up in the morning and extremely difficult to function normally through the day.
- ***Hurting Themselves:*** Some people even harm themselves because they are being bullied. This is called self-harming. People may self-harm by cutting their skin and pulling at their hair, even tugging out strands of it. They may hit hard objects to hurt themselves and scratch their skin. They sometimes burn or pinch themselves. Tragically, some people become so desperate and depressed as a result of their bullying that they commit suicide, or take their own lives.

IT HAPPENED TO THEM

One especially tragic case of bullying involved 14-year-old Adriana Kuch from New Jersey, who died by suicide in 2023 after being attacked at school. A video of the attack was shared online, leading to further bullying and public humiliation. This tragic event highlights the dangers of both physical and online bullying. Victims of bullies can face constant abuse both in person and through technology, and the pressure of such an onslaught can be overwhelming.

> Tragically, some people ... take their own lives.

PROBLEMS AT SCHOOL AND COLLEGE

Bullying has serious and far-reaching impacts for people in both school and college. It can severely affect their academic performance. Bullying can also have long-reaching consequences that can affect people into adulthood.

Bullying can severely affect someone's ability to concentrate, which damages their schoolwork.

SPOILING SCHOOL

Bullying at school is harmful in many ways, not least the effect it has on a student's performance at school. Teens who are bullied struggle with a number of issues at school, including:

- ***Problems with Focus:*** When teens experience bullying, it can have a big effect on their ability to concentrate. As a result, teens often struggle to carry out school or college work. Research has shown that bullied teens often experience a drop in grades and struggle with concentration.
- ***Skipping School:*** Fear of facing bullies may lead to increased absenteeism, or failing to go to school. In some cases, teens will start to skip classes, or whole schooldays, so they can avoid the bullies. This can mean that they fall behind with schoolwork and get into trouble with teachers. That may mean they do not do as well in school as they deserve to.
- ***Dropping Out:*** Chronic bullying can cause teens to become so distressed that they decide the only way they can cope is to take themselves out of the situation altogether, and drop out of school.

According to the National Center for Educational Statistics (NCES), 15 percent of students who are bullied skip school at least once during the year.

IT HAPPENS

Some teens may respond to bullying with aggression. People who react to bullying in this way may go on to bully others. They are often known as "bully-victims," because they are both victims of bullies and bullies themselves. Their aggressive behavior can lead to them becoming isolated from other teens. They are also more likely to be disciplined by teachers as a result, which makes their experience at school even worse.

SOCIAL AND EMOTIONAL DAMAGE

Teens who are bullied also suffer in social and emotional ways at school or college. The harmful effects of bullying often cause them to withdraw from others and become more distrustful of their peers. Bullied teens often show these social and emotional problems:

- ***Difficulty with Making Friends:*** Bullied teens may have trouble developing trusting and supportive relationships with their peers. They may also be perceived as "different," which can lead to even more isolation if they are not accepted by other teens.
- ***Fear of Others:*** Bullying can make teens fearful of social situations, leading to social anxiety disorder (SAD). Teens who are bullied may avoid group activities, clubs, or events at school. That limits their social development and enjoyment of school life.

"I just couldn't face going to school. I knew they'd be there, waiting for me."

Hurting Her Makes Me Feel Better

MONDAY MARCH 24

School was pretty fun today. Shauna just doesn't see it coming. We waited for her at lunch, then asked where she got her outfit from. Maybe a yard sale? It was pretty funny. She does look like she gets dressed in the dark. I'm always really careful when I pick out my clothes. Mom tells me I look a state most days, so I don't want to give her more ammunition. And I don't want anyone at school having a reason to get at me too. You can't give people any chance to find a hole. That's where Shauna goes wrong. She asks for it, really.

WEDNESDAY APRIL 9

I took a photo of Shauna at the mall today. She was fiddling with her hair and looked really dumb. And she was right underneath a giant ice-cream poster. I captioned the pic: Too many of those will make you look like this!

I hate my life, hate being here, hate everything.

Then I posted it online. Got loads of likes and responses. A couple of losers said I was mean, and to stop it. Who cares what they think?

THURSDAY JUNE 12

Mom slapped me this morning. She is so mean. I said, what is that for? She said I didn't clean up yesterday, and I'm disrespectful. She can talk. The place is a pit, and she is always horrible to me.

I feel so mad inside, like I hate everyone. They are all out to get you, and if you aren't the toughest, someone else will be. And they'll make you suffer. That's why you've got to be on top—always.

When I saw Shauna, I still felt mad so I put out a foot and she tripped over. Her bag shot across the hall and her glasses went flying. She looked like an idiot! Hurting her makes me feel better. Like I'm in control. Ellie and Julie laughed—they think I'm really funny. I saw a couple of other kids just stare at me, though. That made me feel weird. A bit later, I saw Shauna was crying. Maybe I felt a bit bad, but I didn't let anyone see. They'd just think I'm weak.

FRIDAY JUNE 20

Mom has been screaming and yelling at me tonight. Telling me I'm an ugly, ungrateful loser kid. Said she wished she'd never had me, and I ruined her life. She pulled my hair really hard, and said I needed to start helping out more around the house or I'm out.

I hate her. I wish I could get out of here, I'd go tomorrow if I had any money.

WEDNESDAY JUNE 25

Mrs Harris called me in to her office today. I knew it had to be something bad. When the school principal calls you in, you know it's serious. And I'm not exactly her favorite student. She told me there had been bullying complaints about me. She says they will be investigating, and monitoring me. Mrs Harris said that I also need to go to see the school counselor, to talk things through. Talk what through? Talking never fixes anything. Nothing ever gets better for me ...

CHAPTER FOUR

DEALING WITH BULLYING

Managing teen bullying starts with always talking about it. Bullies hope that the people they are bullying will keep quiet, so they can carry on hurting them without any resistance. When people who are bullied speak up and tell others what is happening, the wall of silence is broken and the bully's power to harm their victim begins to fade. Talking with a trusted adult is always the first step in dealing with bullying. That person might be a parent or caregiver, another family member, or a teacher, for example.

INVOLVING SCHOOLS

A lot of teen bullying takes place at school, in which case the school needs to be told about what is happening. Today, many schools have anti-bullying policies. People such as teachers, counselors, or principals are trained in how to manage bullies and bullying at school. They come up with solutions to deal with the bullying, and put a plan in place.

KEEPING EVIDENCE

Having evidence that bullying has taken place is really important in helping to stop it. By keeping a record of times, dates, and accounts of what happened during bullying, teens can show that to adults. They can then use that information to stop the bullying. Keeping a record of people who have witnessed the bullying also helps. A trusted adult can then talk to them and use that information to further deal with the bullying.

People who are being bullied often worry that they will be teased for "snitching." In fact, bullies often rely on that, knowing that the fear will keep their victims from speaking out.

TAKING BACK CONTROL

Teens can also take personal action to deal with bullies. The best **tactic** when faced with a bully is to ignore them. It is tempting to want to answer back, or even fight back, especially if the bullying has been going on for a while. But it is important to remember that a reaction is exactly what a bully wants. By ignoring them, it stops them from getting the satisfaction of a response. They want to see an angry or upset reaction. When that doesn't come, the bullying becomes less rewarding for them.

IT HAPPENED TO THEM

Singer-songwriter Camila Cabello was bullied at school after moving to the United States from Cuba. She says she was teased about her accent and for being different, and struggled to fit in with other teens at her school. Since becoming famous, Camila has spoken out about the importance of showing kindness. She also talks about how important it is to find confidence within as a teenager, and to be proud of your identity and where you come from.

Only 46 percent of students who are bullied at school report it. Many do not report bullying because they fear they will not be taken seriously. They may also worry that if they do report their bullying, and a teacher talks to the bully about it, it could make the situation even worse. It is important to remember that, today, most schools have strict anti-bullying policies. They are in place to ensure there is no fallout from reporting bullying and that victims are taken seriously and protected.

FIGHTING BACK AGAINST CYBERBULLYING

Cyberbullying can be anonymous, and that can make it more difficult to get evidence about cyberbullies. However, even if bullies use false names, everything that is posted on the Internet stays there. That still is true, even if a bully deletes a post. When a file has been uploaded, it goes onto a server so it can be viewed later. And it stays on the server. So, if a bully posts mean messages or upsetting images online, someone will be able to find them and use them as evidence. For a bully, the other danger is that in the future, an employer will be able to see their activity when they apply for a job. Their behavior will be a concern, and could stop them from getting jobs.

KEEPING SAFE ONLINE

Cyberbullying is a horrible, **toxic** way to behave. However, there are actions that people can take to help protect themselves against online bullying:

- ***Phone Protection:*** A cell phone number should only be given out to friends and family that are trusted. That number should never be passed on to anyone else without permission.
- ***Blocking Unknown Callers:*** It is also important that people only answer calls from people they know. Calls from withheld numbers should never be taken, and replies to texts or other messages from unknown people should never be sent.

Cyberbullying is extremely harmful and destructive.

- ***Safeguarding Information:*** People can keep safe by not giving out personal information when chatting or posting online. That information includes an email address, phone number, and passwords. People should never give these personal things (including their home address) to anyone who is not already a friend or a member of their family.
- ***Not Responding:*** Not replying to unpleasant emails or postings in chatrooms means that bullies are not engaged with.
- ***Using an Alternative Name:*** In some online situations, using a fake name provides some protection. For example, it means if bullying does take place by one or more people in a chatroom, it is easy to simply leave. It also means that the bullies cannot find you again.
- ***Keeping Chats Private:*** Setting up private chatrooms or groups that include only friends who know and trust each other is another way to keep out the bullies.

IT HAPPENS

Sometimes, bullies do manage to get hold of people's numbers, perhaps first pretending to be friendly, then behaving in a bullying way once they have access to a person's phone. If someone does start to bully by text, it is important that they are not replied to. The best reaction to a bully is no reaction. If a bully does not get a response, they are more likely to just give up. However, if that doesn't happen, their number should be blocked. Report the bullying to an adult too. Phone companies can also trace the number of someone who sends abusive messages.

The best reaction to a bully is no reaction.

KEY WAYS TO DEAL WITH PARENTAL BULLYING

Dealing with a parent who is a bully is really hard. After all, for most teens, their parents are the people they would usually turn to for help. Although it can feel difficult to deal with parental bullying, it is important to tackle it. Teens can begin by explaining to their parents that the way they are behaving is making them feel bad and is hurting them.

SPEAKING UP ABOUT UPSETTING BEHAVIOR

Parents may not even realize what they are doing and how it is making their children feel. They may just believe they are encouraging their kids to work harder at school, for example, while the way they are doing so is actually putting down the teen. They may be having their own problems, perhaps at work, and taking those problems out on their kids. Bullying isn't right, whatever the reason for it. But parents are human, just like everyone else. Sometimes, they don't behave as well as they should.

Talking to parents about their behavior is the first thing to do. In many instances, they will likely listen, and hopefully change their behavior. But if this is not the case, teens may need to find another trusted adult to talk to. That might be a different family member, teacher, or their doctor.

Bullying should never be tolerated, no matter who the bully is. It is important that teens feel that they can take action and protect themselves.

DEALING WITH OTHER ADULT BULLIES

Bullying by anyone is wrong and should be stopped—even if that person is someone in authority, such as a teacher or a coach. It is important to challenge all forms of bullying, because bullying can have a toxic effect on those who witness it too—making them think it is acceptable to treat people that way, and perhaps bully themselves. If a teen feels they are being bullied by an adult at school, they should talk to their parents or caregivers. They need to explain what is happening, and ask them to talk to the teacher or coach. Ensuring that they are keeping up with homework, class projects, or practice sessions also removes any reason to criticize the teen—and any excuse for the bully's behavior.

IT HAPPENS

Sometimes, despite talking to an adult who is bullying, things don't change. In that instance, parents should speak to the principal of the school and even to the school board, until something is done to stop the bullying. There are also some other things that teens can do to help deal with the situation. Having evidence of the bullying, particularly when it is carried out by an adult, can really help. For example, if a sports coach is bullying during practice, parents can video the behavior and then use it to show a school principal. Talking to other teens about what is going on, and asking them if they are experiencing similar behavior is also important. Having the support and evidence from peers makes a case against the adult far more powerful.

Bullying isn't right, whatever the reason for it.

They Always Find Me

FRIDAY JANUARY 17

Today was the worst—they got me after football practice, when no one else was looking. Pushed me up against the lockers and called me every racist name they could think of. Ripped my top. Then Damian hit me, and really hard. They all laughed then. Like it was the biggest joke. Don't tell anyone, Damian called back as they walked away. He said I knew what would happen if I did. I had a spare top, so I put that on before I left. Coach asked if all was OK. Sure, I told him. Nothing he could do, even if he knew what was happening.

SATURDAY MARCH 15

I was at the grocery store today when I saw them waiting outside. I didn't want to go out. I knew they were waiting for me. Mom needed me to do the shopping, so I'd gone. Thought I'd be OK. But they always find me.

I could see the store staff were wondering why I was there for so long. Kept looking at me, like I was going to steal something. I waited as long as I could, then paid for the shopping and left. I ran past them toward the bus, but they were too fast. They got me and pushed me into a side street. Hey, he's got us lunch, they kept laughing.

They ripped the bag off me and took everything out. I asked them not to, to stop it. Said it's for my mom. But they didn't care. They took all the cookies and drinks, then smashed some eggs. Lewis shoved the bag back at me. Run home and tell your mommy, he said. I hate him. Hate him. Hate myself more, though. Why didn't I hit back, yell at them. I'm the loser they say I am.

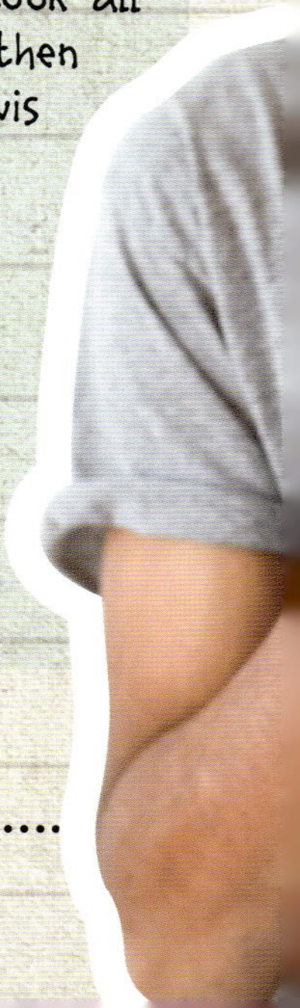

MONDAY JUNE 16

In math class today, they kept flicking things at my head, when Mr Graves was out of the room. Over and over, and laughing all the time. Some of the other kids were laughing too. But I could see Ellis looked really mad. So did Ant. Ellis kept asking me why I didn't say anything. Told him it will only make things worse.

WEDNESDAY JUNE 18

After school, Ellis and Ant walked out with me. Damian and Lewis followed us, so Ellis walked up to them. Ant went with him. Said if they wanted trouble, they'd found it. Said if they touch me, they'll come after them. Ellis and Ant are big guys. No one wants to mess with them. Damian and Lewis looked pretty freaked out at that.

I don't know why Ant and Ellis want to help me. I'm the puny little guy. But they said Damian and Lewis are racist idiots. Ant said his cousin was bullied for being Black. They said they've got my back.

MONDAY JUNE 23

We went into lunch together today. I told Ellis and Ant the whole story about what has been happening over the last few months. Ant said I've got to report it and to tell Coach—he hates racism. They said they'd come with me. So I decided to tell coach.

Coach was really mad. Said those guys are off the team. Then he said he shouldn't have told me that, but it's true. They are out. He says he is taking it all the way, to the principal and school board if needed. I told him that they'll come after me. He said let him take care of that. Said I need to trust him. Ant said Coach will handle it. Just got to wait and see what happens next.

I feel like I should fight back. But I'm scared. And that makes me feel even worse.

CHAPTER FIVE

GETTING OVER BULLYING

As with all deeply upsetting experiences, getting over bullying takes time and a lot of patience. Bullying eats away at a person's self-esteem, self-confidence, and self-perception. If the bullying has gone on for a while, it can take time to rebuild a feeling of self-worth once more. Many teens who have gone through bullying say that some key tools helped them get past the experience and begin to rebuild their lives.

SURROUNDED BY SUPPORT

Seeking support from family and friends is very important. Being surrounded by people who know about the bullying, and who are supportive and encouraging, helps teens speak about what has happened and feel that they are not alone. Bullying can be a very isolating experience, and people often turn inward as a result and become very withdrawn. Having a supportive group of friends and family who are there to listen when someone wants to talk, or just put an arm around them when they feel low, helps to break that isolation. It makes them feel that they are not on their own with their problems.

*Teens often develop greater emotional **resilience** and coping tools as a result of therapy to treat the trauma of bullying.*

IT HAPPENS

Sadly, sometimes teens shut down after they have been bullied and may find it extremely difficult to talk about what has happened to them. They may try to block out the experience and pretend that it never happened. However, tying to pretend something bad never happened doesn't work. People often find that acknowledging they have been a victim of bullying, and that the experience was painful and destructive, helps them. It allows them time and space to work through difficult feelings and begin to get past them. It also helps them begin to recognize that the bullying was never their fault and they did not deserve it.

TALKING ABOUT IT

If teens have been deeply affected by bullying, they may benefit from talk therapy with a trained therapist to help them work through their feelings. Therapy provides a safe space for people to talk about what has happened and express their feelings. Teens may experience many different emotions after the bullying has ended, from sadness and depression to anger and a feeling of self-blame. Therapists can help them work through these difficult feelings and thoughts. Some teens may find it hard to verbally express how they are feeling. In these instances, a therapist can work with them to find another way to show their thoughts and emotions. That may include other forms of therapy, such as art therapy or journaling.

"I found it really hard to talk about it at first. I was ashamed. I felt like I should have been able to protect myself."

REBUILDING AFTER BULLYING

Therapy often helps teens regain a sense of confidence. It also helps them build skills that mean they can better cope with future situations involving confrontation or manipulation. If and when these difficult situations crop up, people are less likely to fall back into past patterns and tolerate the abuse.

THE IMPORTANCE OF SELF-CARE

Self-care is also an important part of recovering from bullying. Caring for oneself is a sign of self-respect and self-worth. When people build self-care into their lives, it reinforces those positive ideas. Self-care can involve taking time to enjoy things, such as a hobby or doing enjoyable exercise. It also means prioritizing one's wellbeing, such as trying to eat healthily. **Mindfulness** and **meditation** in particular can be valuable self-care practices. Many people say they helped them manage the feelings of stress, anxiety, and depression they had to deal with as a result of bullying.

"I now know that I'll never let anyone bully me again. And I'll never stand by while someone else is bullied."

Key to all therapy after bullying is rebuilding a sense of self-worth and self-belief. The majority of young people who go to talk therapy after being bullied say that it improved their self-esteem.

LOOKING FORWARD AGAIN

Rebuilding a sense of enjoyment from activities that may have been put on hold during bullying helps teens look forward to things again. It provides a new focus on positives rather than constantly thinking about when they may next be bullied. Being part of a sports club, or a drama or music club, for example, gives people a sense of normality and helps them realize that the bullying is no longer part of their life. It also means they are more likely to connect with others in a healthy way and therefore avoid feeling isolated and lonely.

FINDING STRENGTH AND FOCUS

Bullying is a horrible experience, and no one should have to go through it. But trying to focus on the positives helps many victims of bullying recover from this traumatic time. Using their experience to help others can be very therapeutic. That can include raising awareness of bullying, joining anti-bullying campaigns, and calling-out bullying if it is witnessed. By empowering themselves with positive actions, teens can help turn a destructive experience into a positive one. Victims of bullying do survive it and go on to build happy and fulfilling lives. And they are often stronger as a result.

Enjoying activities that may have been put on hold when someone was bullied is a healthy part of recovery from the experience.

Research shows that therapy is a powerful recovery tool for bullied teens. About 70–80 percent of teens who experienced bullying and then received therapy found that the anxiety and depression they suffered from were greatly reduced as a result.

No Longer Someone's Victim

AMY'S STORY
MONDAY JULY 21

Tina hasn't been back at school since she was caught. Mrs Cooke told me she has been removed from school while the case is investigated. She said not to worry. I won't be bothered by Tina again.

Over the last few weeks I've started to feel better. I've made friends with the new girl too, Jasmine. We sit together at lunch. Claudia and Jenny came over to talk to us today. They said they are really sorry they didn't do anything to help. They were scared of Tina, and thought if they did anything, she'd start on them. I said it's OK, I get it. We've promised each other that if we see bullying again, we'll call it out—no one should be allowed to bully.

JOE'S STORY
SATURDAY MAY 17

The morning after the conference, Mom said she'd been offered a new job, but it meant a move to South Carolina, back near her family. Then she said, just the two of us—you and me. She kept saying she was really sorry, but I just said, Mom, stop. You don't need to say sorry. He is mean to us both. I love Dad, I mean, I really do. But I don't want to live with him. I want to go.

Amy: I've started writing a story about bullying. Mom says I could try to get it published. That would be amazing.

We went the next week. Since, Mom and I have been seeing a family therapist. He says Dad was abusive. It's hard to hear, but I know it's true. I don't feel so low these days, and I know Dad's behavior wasn't my fault. Mom says it's behind us now, and we'll get strong again, together.

CARLA'S STORY
MONDAY SEPTEMBER 22

School put me on a behavioral intervention plan, and I had to go see the school counselor, Ms Phelps. She spent a lot of time with me, just talking. Kept asking me about Mom. Told her Mom comes and goes, and mostly when she is around, she's pretty mean. Ms Phelps tried to contact Mom, but wasn't able to reach her. She said a social worker was taking over. Then Mom just went one day. I've got no idea where.

When the social worker found out that Mom had gone, I was moved to a shelter, then a foster family. After that, I started therapy. My therapist is great, I really like her. She treats me like a person, not a problem. We talk a lot about Mom, and what I did to Shauna. I feel bad about it now. I was as bad to her as Mom was to me. I don't want to be like that again. Ellie, my therapist, says that is the road to the other side of bullying. She says I'm not a bad person, so does May, my foster Mom. I'm trying to believe them. I want to. I don't want to be like Mom.

KAREEM'S STORY
MONDAY SEPTEMBER 15

After I told Coach, there was an investigation and the teachers interviewed loads of other students. Turns out it wasn't just me Damian and Lewis had got to. Both of them were expelled from school. Since then, everything has been better. I'm not scared anymore that they are waiting for me. I still have bad days when I feel like I'm just this dorky guy that can't do anything. Ant says that's because Damian and Lewis made me feel like that. Says his cousin was the same, but he's much stronger now. It took him a while to get over it, but he says he's looking ahead now. I'm trying to do that too.

GLOSSARY

abuses treats someone in an unacceptable way that harms them physically or emotionally
adolescence part of life between childhood and adulthood
anxiety an intense feeling of worry
depression intense feeling of sadness
disability a physical or mental issue that affects a person's quality of life
empathy an ability to share and understand the feelings of others
hierarchies systems that allocate a level of importance to people within groups
hormonal related to chemical substances that act like messengers in the body
Identity the self-image that a person develops
immune system the system in the body that fights invading bodies such as viruses and harmful bacteria
isolated separated from others
manipulate to exert unhealthy control and influence over someone
meditation a method of calming the mind and bringing about a sense of wellbeing, often using particular breathing and relaxation exercises
mindfulness a method of calming the mind by focusing on the present
Nazis the National Socialist German Workers' Party, a far-right political party led by Adolf Hitler. The Nazis rose to power in Germany during the 1930s
peer pressure pressure from people of a similar age to do something or behave in a particular way
peers people of a similar age and who are experiencing similar things
prejudice a negative opinion of a person or group of people that is not based on actual fact
psychological related to the mind and a person's thoughts and feelings
puberty a period of great hormonal change that changes a body from a childlike form into an adult
resilience the ability to quickly recover from disappointment or setback and keep moving forward
self-esteem confidence in one's abilities
stress a feeling of extreme tension
swastikas symbols in the form of a black cross with each arm bent at a right angle
tactic an action taken to achieve a specific goal
taunting talking to someone in an unkind way in order to upset them and get a response
tension mental and emotional stress
terrorist a person who uses violence or threat of violence to achieve their political goals
tolerate to accept
toxic has a negative, harmful effect
trauma a very difficult experience that leaves lasting damage
turban a head covering made of a long length of material wound around the head

FIND OUT MORE

BOOKS

Benson, Jodyanne. *Bullying* (@RosenTeenTalk). Rosen Publishing Group, 2021.

Knabb, Muriel. *Teens Dealing with Online Bullying* (Teens Dealing with Adversity). ReferencePoint Press, 2025.

Rockler, Naomi. *Challenges for Teen Girls: Anxiety, Self-Image, and Bullying.* ReferencePoint Press, 2024.

WEBSITES

For key facts about bullying and help to deal with it visit:
https://dosomething.org/article/11-facts-about-bullying

Learn more about bullying, how to deal with it, and why people bully at:
https://kidshealth.org/en/teens/bullies.html

Find out more about bullying and what you can do to take action against it at:
https://pacerteensagainstbullying.org

Discover more actions to take to stop bullying at:
www.stopbullying.gov/resources/teens

ORGANIZATIONS

That's Not Cool
Website: www.Thatsnotcool.com
24-hour hotline (1-866-331-9474)
If you or someone you know is experiencing bullying, you can reach out to this online resource about bullying. It also provides information about relationship abuse and peer pressure.

PUBLISHER'S NOTE TO EDUCATORS AND PARENTS:

All the websites featured above have been carefully reviewed to ensure that they are suitable for students. However, many websites change often, and we cannot guarantee that a site's future contents will continue to meet our high standards of educational value. Please be advised that students should be closely monitored whenever they access the Internet.

INDEX

ABOUT THE AUTHOR

Sarah Eason has written many books for children and young adults, including a number of social and emotional support books. She hopes this book will provide young people with useful information about bullying, and support young people trying to deal with this painful problem.